Paper Pavilion

■ ■ ■

For Aunt [...]
Much love to
you. I'm
so proud
of you!

PAPER PAVILION

■■■

JENNIFER KWON DOBBS

The White Pine Press Poetry Prize

WHITE PINE PRESS / BUFFALO, NEW YORK

Published by
White Pine Press
P.O. Box 236
Buffalo, New York 14201
www.whitepine.org

The White Pine Press Poetry Prize
Volume Number 12

First Edition

Acknowledgements
Thank you to the editors of the following publications, in which some of this work previously appeared, sometimes in versions with other titles.: *5 AM*, *The Cimarron Review*, *Crazyhorse*, *The Cream City Review*, *MiPOesias Magazine*, *Poetry NZ*, *The Tulane Review*, and the anthologies *Echoes Upon Echoes* (Temple University Press, 2003) edited by Elaine Kim and Laura Hyun Yi Kang and *Contemporary Voices from the Eastern World* (W.W. Norton & Co., 2007) edited by Tina Chang and Ravi Shankar. Thank you to Bob Bryan of Bryworld Productions and Jan Beatty and Ellen Placey Wadey of Prosody 91.3 WYEP.

Cover image: Detail of an early 19th Century Korean painting by Hyewon (Sin Yun-bok, b. 1758) depicting a female entertainer performing a sword dance .

13-digit ISBN 978-1-893996-90-8

Printed and bound in the United States of America

Library of Congress Control Number: 2007937845

for my parents

Contents

"The moon shines on Cold Pine Pavilion

. . .

why is it that our beloved prince,
once gone, is never to return?"
— Hongjang
(undated)

A Small Gift

Ku Sang, guide me as a tender brother
scrupulous with pathways
to the Han
that flows above the sky.

Below hanging baskets of ivy
in the shadow of tenements,
I spend my light counting sorrows
the ants haul across railings.

Let me listen to your chest's easy crests,
falling and rising
to take your shirt's hem.

Let me collect the button and thread
about to unravel.

I'll show you,
when you awaken,
how I shellacked them with ox blood
for a pendant charm.

And you will sternly correct me
by touching my face
as you would a mirror
the river becomes in autumn morning.

And you will say in Korean
something I'll feel without translation
run through me a current
of sadness mixed with some joy.

I.

"Our destination is fixed on the perpetual motion of search.
Fixed in its perpetual exile."
— Theresa Hak Kyung Cha

Homage to the DMZ

Guards, please keep your triggers locked.
My camera, maps, and pick are left behind.

No spy, I do not come to break the code
Nor tour the warning walls. No uncle waits

To reunite across electric wire,
To touch my face and call it true to his

One memory: the burning trees and mud-
Caked women running in the hazy night.

No memories, but still my grief has skin
And hands to comb the Han with nets cast deep

And hands to comb the Han with nets cast wide
And lips to speak my peace. I can't recall

The distant whistling growing louder when
It flashed across the dark, careened, then boomed

And echoed in the crash of pummeled walls
Collapsing in the strobe-lit dark, while late

Alarms began to wail of fighter jets
Diving low in rows for gunner range.

I wasn't with the people trapped inside
Mistaken targets; throngs of people fled,

Ignored the old ones stumbling, children, parts
Of bodies hurled with rubble, shrapnel pierced

Debris, and smoke. A sister stopped to check
Her brother slipping down her back and strapped

To his, a kettle came untied and spilled.
Its grain was lost to sludge, cold and chance,

The midnight raids on fallout shelters smashed
By aircraft, tanks forever on the move

To battle fronts while people streamed against
Advancing troops to safety. Where was that?

It's hard to tell when lines deployed in all
Directions, rivers soured by floating fish.

Yet hunger had to eat, examined hair for lice,
Dug roots and worms. The stench of shit and muck,

The stains of vomit, rags bound tight to stop
The spread of gangrene, sores mosquitoes sucked

Or numbed by fever's spell, exposed, each eye
Ahead on sunset, nights of transit, hush.

The people wound through hills till nitrous gas
Lashed their faces peeled to bone. They shone

Absurdly white in morning fields of charred
Anemone awaiting help, return,

Some sign. "I'll find you" promised. No one could
Identify their paths by what remained.

Missing children hid inside ravines
Or crept outside their hiding place to search

The ruins, found a metal strip and bent
It back-and-forth into a knife to fend

Off men who tried to snatch the can of food
That they had stolen as a barefoot gang,

Or stayed beside her broken body spread
Into a shape of loss I cannot trace

To find her soldier-lover marching south
Or husband killed in action. Nameless men

Forced themselves upon her, cupped some snow
To pack a ball inside her pleading mouth?

I can't go on, can't imagine how
She bore this child though I could be that child

Of mixed-up rivers, hard attempts to keep
A secret. Why return to unknown names

I feel are mine when snipers watch this ground?
While they remain, how can I begin?

LETTER TO OKLAHOMA (1)

I've got to go or I'll suffocate
in so much space. I fear
your dead-end dirt roads.

I chart a way out of this zodiac
of backyard trash fires.
Your water is undrinkable.

Everyone spits dust
that clots screened in porches.
Inside, I read *The World Book,*

contemplate volume A's "anteater"
for other than myself
reflected in your sky like a stadium

mirror for copper rusted posts,
guarding trucks engines fell out of.
I need skyscrapers

to hem back your night's fabric,
some florescence other than moon,
but you enfold me in Indian paintbrushes,

shadow me with willows
giving in to wind free from limits.
I would give thanks

to sod removed block by block for shelter,
a passage of hands,
exposed taproot breaking the tools.

I came so close to calling this
wound of ground a home,
but it felt too familiar.

Aria for Slag & Embers

"Vissi d'arte. Vissi d'amore."
— Giacomo Puccini, *La Tosca*

I'm not supposed to know how
my father does this every night.

With a pocketknife, he slices his heel
calluses to feel the new underneath,

gathers the yellow peels into a pile,
drops them into an ashtray, loads the pipe,

then sucks the cherry to glow.
It steals his breath. He is used to this

tenderness, this post graveyard shift habit.
He settles into smoke, does not imagine

it's like the furnace fumes that cloak
the cauldron named "Our Lady"

swinging above the workers below
who ready the rock tundish.

No secret offerings. They glove
their hands out of necessity. They bring

only wire to scrape
the cast hole for the molten to pass.

It pours into molds; glows like the tabernacles,
like saving hatreds, like ledger columns.

Like an idol, it demands loans of the spirit
it will never pay back, wants children to believe

books should be returned on time.
I hang on to see

my father in the center of an imploded star,
flipping on the t.v. & skipping past reruns.

He pauses before a broadcast on Orion & stares
at the bright belt hung in the sky,

raised club to strike the invisible
tracking the hunter.

My father draws the remote
from the recliner, makes no conclusions.

Shirtless, pink, he leans toward the flickering
form & is always, as I shall recall,

painted by sparks, slag burning off,
his shadow thrown everywhere

in the desire to live for art & love.
If I could suspend this moment,

I could touch his raw steel,
but he has worked all day on this

to the usual. He is shirtless, pink.
His tobacco embers cool.

ELEGY FOR DANIEL

(1970-2001)

After the bullet discharges through the tunnel of his mouth,
    after it shatters

the Oklahoma evening, rips through ragweed & across many rivers,
    my apartment in Pittsburgh,

the metal clips my arm, slams into a plaster wall,
    & the silence is his

body slackening & the black fact of the gun underwater.

I compress my wound as his ghost kneels beside his body,
    the bathtub, &
        as his ghost draws the shower curtain back,

I look away. No, I don't want to know his secrets, why
    surer hands will tag, bag as evidence.

He is a poet. He makes the difficult question of speaking
    a matter of remembering
        how he shouted the poems he loved.

His outbursts were pure country. Yes, rumors circulated,
    how vets suffer

medication, what he saw as a S.E.A.L., how weird,
    & no one could stand
        the belabored way he read aloud,

& I said all the above & more, & to his face
    when no one was around when he finally caught on,

I asked him, 'Why are you quieter? I've noticed, & it scares me.'

*

Even now I'm busy with details, the dirty work of gathering.

Here's rosemary & some pansies, that's for thoughts
   rambled to me one Fall afternoon, Cathedral of Learning,

how Komunyakaa showed him a way to anchor a moment
   between stillness & approach

turning toward tall grass or a woman's wet hair to braid,
   or how it could lock arms with an enemy,

lose to an overwhelming grasp, or listen to the dying
   echo of paradise birds singing

so much gibberish, as if a whole life could be reduced to one image
   dangling from a fist & engraved with a number,

as if a poem wants only to be identified upon delivery,
   which was why Daniel read Blake,

Calvino & Crane for fire & crystal. Why he shut himself up
   with Bishop. Why Stern's huge breath,

why Oppen, Tu Fu & Paz. Lewis & Vollmer mattered
   for their generosities, lines layered like the earth
     in his face,

the reds & browns of his voice deepening to what he pursued,
    half-formed in haze

& burrowing underneath to avoid tripwire, & Daniel yelling as he
    plunged after its gray, disappearing shape.

*

I listen to his ghost pace the hallway as if barefoot across dirt,
    fronds like unfurled scrolls, rustle.

Root scent & rainfall stain his cheeks with welcome, risk.
    He has walked far to finish this conversation between us.

He brushes against the wood, taps the doorknob trying to explain
    the jagged web of cracks in my wall,

hot metal at the center like a labyrinth chamber
    or the slick tip of a widow

hunched over & spinning a bundle or the pure ore from a journey
    toward sublimation, a soul's treasure,

or the soul, itself, lodged in a network & inconsolable
    because wings never guaranteed perfect pitch.

*

Daniel, the scar on my arm fades as I read your poems again,
    & the maps you drew

time spackles over for a move out west.

The twenty that someone taped to my office desk for flowers
        remains unspent,
                a bookmarker for a Ramses biography.

I tried I couldn't find your permanent address.

Daniel, the news today proclaims disaster, code orange to survive
        for tomorrow's headline

that you were right could, at any moment, slip under a thicket,
        emerge skittish beside a pile of leaves,

its long gray nose & black eyes focused on your movements.

How you wrote it down, my friend, held it
        in the starless night
                & gave it pink fingers with which to scratch back.

.

Libretto

*"Non saperlo per te, pei tuoi puri occhi
muore Butterfly..."*
— Giacomo Puccini, *Madama Butterfly*

Again, my false mother of verbena is singing

The aria that I'll recite as if I'm a natural

Child among night flowers opening their dark eyes to the moon

Not a mother to the ocean that bears its resemblance

Like a floating summer barge. Again, I am sinking into her

Hazardous silks of caged birds and mute crickets, into her

Televised longing for smoke stacks and flags, into her image

Painted on to a soprano's face, into her vermilion

Folds in which are sealed the purposes, provisional

Names for my hands dragging a brass opener through wax.

The dream drips on to the table, makes new forms

All scraped and discarded. Beginning is always a problem

When toenail, strand of hair, some notes

Scribbled by a social worker in a code familiar as skin:

Where is my baby? Is my baby hungry?

Does she mourn as I do? Is this loss or libretto?

What is our contract, if there is blood between us? Have I the right

To scabs picked for pink underneath, little shutters to let in air,

The pure music. It is raw in there. I am guessing

An alcove to grieve among robes embroidered with cherry blossoms,

festival wagons, cranes returning to a patch of silver at the breast,

Leave-taking. Every sleeve, myth. Every hem, a crossing

Guarded by dust, dry creek beds, buffalo grass, sky like a kiln.

Not the blue heat, but the orange as in tiger lily, the yellow foxglove

Seed ground into the heart's medicine to quicken

In want of a memory. I was 10, a watcher of things winged,

PBS, Sunday Afternoon at the Met, Levine conducting.

Plastic swatter in hand, my palms against glass to get through.

Windows of my parents' living room covered with damask.

I imagined she called to me, *non saperlo . . . per te,* across a sea

Of bad reception. I did not see myself but heard flies humming.

I studied the white parts squirming out of their black, mashed bellies

In wonder of death. Still, a birth through the wound

Willed by itself. Why else such a distance crossed from its mother

Lying on the wood, her ash veil falling away?

II.

"Men can do nothing without the make-believe
of a beginning."
— Horace, *Ars Poetica*

In Medias Res

0
Muscles bear down, grip instead of push the suspended midway

1
that will become

2
when forceps reach through to drag me, headfirst & unharmed,

3
into a clearing, the ticking, halogen light, the typical

4
slap to spit out fluid, suck in cold air

5
to survive as another image held above her slack form, lying on the
metal table,

6
& cut so that the cord snaps back inside her body. Hands pass me

7
to others that carry me down an arterial hallway without consider-
ing that too an act of delivery. No chance of stopping each
transaction from blurring,

8
how hands rub out with pine scent. The impulse to return & to
want to see that instant,

9
her body in that instance

10
surrounded by assembly & to elbow my way through to find her

11
not like a fish or an unnamed beloved in a yellow dress, but to
check whether she

12
exists as more than evidence

13
or a single brainstorm:

14
Did she blink her eyes or move side-to-side to catch a glimpse? Did
she ask my sex or lie mute? How old was she? Could she afford this?

15
Did she know that I lived?

16
Did she consider me dead? Did she

17
already write my story, disassemble me bit by bit according to the
days that I grew a foot, thumb, ear, & every bone & blood detail

18

until only a sheet thrown over the metal table bore a trace of our relation?

19

It weighs nothing. Each conjecture. I put down the pen & pick it back up. It weighs nothing. I touch the page & then it's true

20

every device wants a vertebrae & a staircase

19

to descend with applause for small accomplishments. I could be wrong because I need her on that metal table or

18

now surrounded by traffic noise in a two-bedroom flat. She hums & thinks nothing of me. Nothing at all.

17

She found a husband at a lunch café in Seoul & created a family. She never looked back

16

the way the living must to make a way. This is not right or wrong.

15

This is just a story,

14

or her rushing upstairs with a briefcase & sack of bread. Her sitting, signing letters & checks.

13

Her signature everywhere & everything bearing her trace.

12

Every trace wanting her more

11

talking with confidence

10

like an image turning to her across a distance & laughing

9

about a summer matinee & slipping

8

an arm through hers to guide across a busy street. No one caring.
No one noticing at all, & why should they

7

when this image is hers, only younger & mine,

6

leaning in

5

to whisper against her gray hair,

4

against her

3
paper thin cheek, & my lips

2
& my lips against

1
the ineffable

0
hollow of her ear?

Painted Fire

Ohwon copied "Party by the Lotus Pond"
        locked in his employer's brass-hinged cabinet,

which he polished everyday with root oil

except once when someone forgot to latch it
        & Ohwon could not resist

opening the doors a little more.

So identical his version that the yangban accused him
        first of theft, then of genius

not befitting an orphan drifter who didn't know his age.

Rumor summoned him to a springtime pavilion
        where the aristocrats gathered

ignoring the new kisaengs' raspberry wine.

        The challenge, a poem composed for the event:

The vast earth and high mountains increase my will to fly.
Withered maples and falling leaves heighten my spirit.

He needed no outline, no bones for his eagle
        rapidly alighting from ink brush to paper,

feather by bristling feather as with searching
        for the thicker part of a branch.

The bird steadying its rippling weight above the vast
      empty field,

clutching & unclenching the phantom twig.
      A wash of ink leaves trembling

as Ohwon's bristles streaked clear, his body like the eagle
      circling the maple

to fasten roots to the rock face, then sitting on his knees
      as a twin appeared below

anchored & armed with a black-eye.

The audience murmured among one another, how was this possible?
      He followed but broke Su Shih's aphorisms.

In Ohwon's one brushstroke, a thousand
      transgressions & with each one, an increase in a will to fly!

LETTER TO OKLAHOMA (2)

The rumor is a plain is a good place to discover
how urban glare interrupts the speech of stars,

yet no one listens to their cadence,
Sousa's "March of Venus,"
or studies the planet's positions to foretell

the right time to kill witch grass by boiling water

so that stars persist, large in their orbits,
as riveted stations in an antique ornament
strung & clasped around a mannequin's neck.

I don't believe in creation as *a priori*,
a wind sweeping over the face of the waters,

or in a formless void that others say delivered me.

Even the ineffable writes as it burns the edge
where heaven meets earth
dragging its foxtail over sage for smoke & ash,

so that nothing is lost, only sent down,
a basket retrieved among reeds & renamed
"I drew him from the river,"

& the silence embracing him loves
thus it conceals every detail of his birth as a slave.

& I'm thinking, we carry a trace worn casually
as an impression

like the lips' bowed cleft
where an angel's finger rested to seal a promise

not to recall the terms by which we're cut loose

vulnerable as the veins in a moth's wings that defy
the pinned shape of surrender

or release, or it's guesswork
we must copy, disobey, then reinvent.

& though the plainness of a day strips each answer
like paint from a barn torn down to a frame,

there are vistas through the frame

& someone young trespassing at twilight,
rushing to stake a claim.

RED

I remain in your leave-taking
like the mandolin's note. Long and lingering

perfume of petals enfolds my body
because you desired me in a red

aura of candles, then clouded by
your palms seeking my origins in cities

you traveled in search of Lorca
finding sandalwood uncurling

like a ghost in a room darkened by blinds.
Above the bright shouts of women bargaining for meat,

we stole from one another silver and pearls,
demanded retribution in bracelets.

May the bruised jewels your lips left me
last the length of your absence.

Will you ask to see me again so adorned?
Or will you bring saffron to stain our bed orange?

Sijo

The necks of the chrysanthemums bow to a passing of days,
Then release mauve petals that I'll press between white leaves
To slip into your lap, when you open this book.

KAMEOKA

Because I dreamed it, I believed wholly in my power
        to alter its outline of fallen persimmons.

The trees shadowing Kyorai's house that Basho praised
        for "bedding and relishes brought over from Kyoto"

spoke in a rustling of branches. "This is Korea,"

I wrote in my journal underneath a sketch of oat grass.

I found repair in every fissure in the scholar's room.
        The shaped infinity felt like homecoming.

It's just that I was so happy that morning in Saga.

Beside the bamboo trellis, I forgot myself completely. I knelt,
        gathered a cake of black dirt, and ate.

✻

A Postcard:

"The Golden Pavilion," reflected in water and seven stories high.
On top, a phoenix with outspread wings poised to take flight.

Dear D— I read that a monk fell so madly in love with the
run-down original that he set fire to it. What you see here is a
reproduction. Which strikes you as more true, story or image?

✻

Within a week, I learn to say, "Excuse me," "yes," and "good morning" with such a proper female inflection that bus drivers no longer greet me or call out my stop.

✻

Japanese Plate—

Fire glazed to preserve my misspelling
my Korean name, some blue accident
of the desire to say, "Here, I was here."

✻

July 29 Kyoto

Wisteria. White lotus in a moonlit pool of water. A split peach design of a *maiko*'s hair slipping as she rushes home from Kiyomizu Temple. Sun goes down as a monk goes down on his knees toward the west, evening sutra on his lips, a chord from the *shakuhachi* ends thin as screensto keep out the light, and inside is the place of myths and makings—

✻

I do not trust stories.
I resist them—

as I would the small
overblown for bric-a-brac—

to unmake the thing into its origins
of sand & heat,

to put my hand in the mess
then draw it out,

& in my hand nothing,
nothing but hot.

✻

While Watanabesan folds the violet *yukata* across my chest, I notice
a small freckle underneath her left eye like mine. "Please," she says,
"call me *okasan*."

✻

On pale green paper, I write: "thank you, *okasan*, for the pickled
cherries."

✻

Flying across the Pacific, I close the window shade.

Beside me, a student sleeps. Wherever he descends after dreaming,
his *Lost Japan* is turned over to hold a place.

I dislike that book's fanciful ache, "looking
for a castle" in a land "that seemed inhabited by gods."

Because Korea, my lost castle, land of my birth and longing—

I would come to you as a tourist as I arrive in Japan a tourist
          of *bunraku* puppets, gardens in which to meditate justice,
                    classes on

history still uncertain, and like the ignorant or orphaned,
          I rush headlong

into a red sun that rose over your peninsula, and now over my eyes
          seeking you in all I behold!

III.

"We all live in total ignorance
in the city of Memory. Erased."
— Enrique Lihn, *Paris, Irregular Situation*

PRODIGAL

Even in Korea,
   I long for Korea.

Some fidelity
   to the proper note:

tongue fitting
   as join, as the letter

reminds it to lift
   fire and wood.

So King Sejong
   told the scholars,

"It must kindle
   the people's hearths."

So too my heart
   must strike metal.

These letters:
   sticks, o's I'll glue for

"d" as in "radio."
   The way I say "radio,"

so effortless.
   A water glass

drops sediments.
   This pull to homeland,

no different than gravity
   giving weight to

the simplest task.
   The city shines through

"Give me grapes"
   (my first sentence)

written 20 times in
   the frost-darkened pane

like a recitation
   or many false starts.

I erase with
   a circle of breath

chrome traffic,
   billboards, subway

crowds jostling
   in rush hour,

every shot at
   home reached by

"The Correct Sounds
   To Instruct the People"

delivered on time.
   I can't spell "home."

It's all brushstrokes
  like a bough

split in half
  by indecision, dew lit

bud where my finger
  paused, and I thought

now each one
  is the beginning

to reach outside
  anonymous as in urban

strut past storefronts,
  neon arrow for transfer.

I could stop there,
  but streaks, handprint,

this glass like a trellis
  for love's polemics.

Overgrown or exact
  risk? I could give in,

stand still in awe.
  It's not enough.

The king returned
  to the mountain pavilion

restless with questions
   for holy woodblocks,

ran his lips across
   the grain to impress

the subtle textures
   he could not capture

otherwise. His failure
   wrote, "the ignorant

seek to express,
   but cannot…"

here, a letter. This one,
   a splinter. This one

char to stand in for
   red ornaments, charmed

knots of white cotton.
   Each, a ghost babbling

loss unknotted
   to release into ether.

Even in Korea,
   I long for Korea

to come undone
   as an embroidered robe

across headlights
　　flicker then shadow

leading to sources
　　crumpled, ink-stained.

Train out of Seoul.
　　Train to the mist

hung passageways
　　the king climbed.

Granite. Filament
　　sun burning its last

message to autumn,
　　red cedar-lined

basin of the heart.
　　That too, a letter

smeared, some bracken.
　　I never sought

flare, tectonic shifts
　　for new land

forms jutting toward
　　heaven, the king

saying, "This is holy
　　ground." You

remove shoes anyway
   when entering

private halls, kneel
   to sit among kindred

dragging hot noodles
   quickly by necessity

between bowl and ...
   "Why," servers ask,

"this fork?"
   The king betrayed

Chinese birds
   gathered by ink

stone and graceful,
   those images of ages;

those pictographs, perfect.
   "But," says the king

to worthy dissenters,
   pen-scepters upraised,

"Our ignorant too
   must eat."

Obaji/father . . . other half of the equation. X + Y chromosomes add up to a foreign embassy. A blue suit greets me like a returnee from a long ago war for tea and sandwiches. I ask him whether Confucius had a daughter named Will.

Another false start: "Hive scooped out of nesting an egg. The cardinal preens himself."

Dad. 52. Steelworker. Democrat. Union member. So Okie it's Miam-ah, not Miam-ee. Schlitz if cheaper than Hurricane at the Qwik Stop.

A.   Abandoned by Father X   Mother X

My students read Hahn's *zuihitsu* for her mother. I admire a hurt like that so whole as to taste salty, to smell metallic, and to pass through oneself to find how omoni might've leaned her head against the bookcase when obaji re-shelved the apiary guide.

My lover is absurdly beautiful. He plucks his eyebrows into languid judgments and despises riding the bus. He is a visual artist. Those ugly people distress him.

I send Dad a list of 30 questions. Mom promises to nag him to answer.

Attempt #2: "Ovum. Inside, an embryo knocks against a shell when moved from one place to another. Who shall her? Progress?"

My lover sleeps on his back with his mouth open and legs up. He is Korean. I am totally fascinated.

One of my students submits a *zuihitsu* about his brother, confined to a wheelchair by a drunk driver. My student handles "a semblance of order" well by moving elliptically through fragments. If I tell him, will pride overtake his exquisite rage?

Attempt #3: "Yellow (adj.): jaundiced, tawny, lily-livered. See 'fever.' See 'Dixie cup.'"

Did he leave her when she grew large and unable to conceal irritation? Did he return only when she agreed to screw legs out like a wheelbarrow leaned into and pushed toward the shed?

Maybe it's that his body differs from mine, and I'm drawn to similarity. I pick at the blue birthmark on my arm. How disappointing that my lover's resembles a mud splatter on his inner thigh!

B.   Separated or lost from   Father _____   Mother _____

Will you respond? What of the color orange? I thought of you the other day snoring in your Lazy Boy. Your feet, two brown bears in summer. Remote stuffed in the catfish's fin slung over the armrest, the television chattering about tires and granola.

My lover and I can't get enough of each other. At a café, I scribble on a napkin, "Shall we?" and rise for the bathroom.

I lend my student my copy of Sei Shonagon's *Pillow Book* to study the form. He wants me to explain, but he ought to experience himself.

Father precedes mother categorically in birth records.

My lover asks permission to videotape our sex because, together, we create beauty. This is getting ridiculous.

Did he throw money at her? Did he hold out for a son surrounded by sesame cakes? Did he not wait? Could he not recall her name? Or did he wake sour-mouthed and reach for water? Or did his eye take in the white cotton creek that her form left in the mattress?

Attempt #4: "The egg sizzles like an idea forcing shape. The bright orb is useless."

My student staples a thank you note to his paper. So many dangling modifiers! I guess at his intention.

Against the broken down Ford, my father smokes cheap cherry tobacco. His telescope points toward the North Star as if to navigate a prairie sea.

My lover hunts for shells to place in my windowsills. I wish he wouldn't do that. How we use one another.

Last attempt: Lambs in winter, and this need is.

C. Death of father: <u>unknown</u>   Death of mother: <u>unknown</u>

Obaji/Father, I will pull back that alien skin sheathing your penis to find another like my tender…

AUTHENTICITY

Brother, you poured water into my cupped hands

Your cool slipped through efforts to grasp

What gratitude I felt for this

You understood me to be so named after

As were your ancestors Cash to a cotton farmer

Bills of sale stored in his safety box

Receipts for adoption stuffed in tea canisters

I doubted resembled your irretrievable history

Yet you insisted amnesia drove us both to rummage

To jimmy open basements, vaults of

Microfiche you unreeled to scan for plantation fields in

Old Sussex County. I had none to speak of

"My all," you said of dogwood trees, arid orchard grass

Where your forefathers & foremothers were buried

"Not my home," you said, yet you could return to it

You said, "I returned from it. I could go on"

You board first-class, luggage bulging with equipment

To field across all of Africa, magnetic compass in hand

How you envied my finger on a map of Asia

Korea. "Your there," you called it

That someone something once upon a time

THE PUPPET MAKER

"Might it be that this piece of wood has learned to weep and cry like a child?"
— C. Collodi, *The Adventures of Pinocchio*

As he angled the screw into the joint
he hesitated to fasten its knee

more real than his own stiffened by winters,

nights of hearth & plates of black bread
that taught gratitude for the small

callous on his forefinger cushioning a day's work.

The puppet in his lap flailed its string-less arms
as if they were given

without fire in mind & the limitless distance

between it & it; yet he
listened not to the reedy voice *I want I want,*

but to the wind thrumming against the shutters,
hollow knock of wood against wood,

a pulse that kept measure with his,

which bored the puppet, so that it leapt & spun away
laughing on its spindle legs

that loosened then splintered, & dragged behind
as it crawled toward him

weeping for repair.

Boy Clown

In my dream, his shadow throws the rubber balls
at Agua Caliente & Avenida Juarez,
so the boy can walk a few paces back
to see the swirling he casts everyday
for coins in a coffee can at his shadow's feet.
There, he can study how to toss faster & higher
to slow the oncoming traffic to surprise,
or he can keep going backward
till the loop seems to burn a white portal
in the summer noon sky &, there, decide
how much further back to go for a good start.
I shall always say I'm lucky to wake
remembering this part. He gets low to the concrete,
pulls his body taut, & tucks his lean arms close.
Then he sprints & leaps through the open
door above the cars past his shadow below.

DOLL IN THE ERMINE CAP

She stands at the edge of rupture,
where the train will plunge into the lake
then rise back on track to loop again.

The doll withstands steel, rumble, pistons, seams.
Her blue glass pools hold the oncoming
riveted face. It will pass through.

She is some longstanding desire
to imitate motion, or she searches
for the cause of trains or an opening

of snowflake arms to embrace
as the black wheels howl through.
Her green skirt ripples. Her auburn curls ring.

As her head tilts back
as by an invisible string, her bud lips part.
Something like a train sounds forth.

IV.

"But home is the form of the dream, & not the dream."
— Larry Levis

FACE SHEET

"I the undersigned, hereby certify
I have custody of the records of birth
Relating to said child, in my office
And as required by the law."
— Livingstone Adoption Agency

Confucius can't spank me with a bamboo switch. I've folded paper cranes
for your journey here, learned Hangul from tutors so that I can greet you,

Father's Name: No Records. Mother's Name: No Records.
Father's Residence: No Records. Mother's Residence: No Records.

omma, studied my face in the mirror — piecing together clues: this
flat nose, pointy chin are yours; these high cheekbones, brows are father's.

*Face Sheet for Child: Legitimate ____ Illegitimate ____ Foundling -_X_*
Distinguishing marks, features: ____ She is peevish. She takes 500 cc's milk.

My mother joked I ran into the wall, squished my head, slanted my eyes. Said
My mother was a slut, trying to stay in business. I was bad for business. Said

She controls her neck & bowel movements well. Abandoned by:
Father: _X-_ Mother: _X_ Include here guardian's attitudes and motives in

I was lucky not to end up a slut too or dead. Said you didn't name me,
so I'm not under contract. No agreements were made or terms defined us.

Releasing child: President Kim would like the baby in a nice home.
$450 Payable, Dec. 76. Remarks/File No. ____ Child's attitude toward: N/A.

The Hidden Aria

> (With a weak gesture, Butterfly points to her child and
> dies. Pinkerton kneels down beside her, while Sharpless
> goes to pick up the child.) END
> — Giacomo Puccini, *Madama Butterfly*

Now that ushers lower & extinguish the chandeliers
& the satin-gowned crowd retires for ices,

now that someone sweeps while crews wheel the sets to storage,

now that violin cases click shut & chorus gossip fades
out the stage door, now dark & the echo

of the janitor's key locking up.

Now he emerges from his hiding place & ascends the stage
to continue the opera

beyond paper screens, a white kimono & a long black wig
dragging the floor as she clutches the blade

singing the words her child, now a young man in cuff links,
recites per his voice training:

...*senza che ti rimorda ai di maturi/ il materno abbandono.*

His name is Sorrow because she will not return
from his father's burned score notes, journals & photographs.

His name is *Tu? tu? tu? & piccolo iddio.*

& "Christopher" to his father's business partners & translated
"My love, my love, flower of the lily and rose."

The bit of orange silk he retrieved from the ash grate
may mean nothing.

He strokes the charred cloth, carried with him
like one faint memory.

She called him *Amore, Amor* as she blindfolded his eyes,
& the aria he cried out from blindness

the music covered with a string crescendo

that so moved the audience; they interrupt even now
thrilled when he tries to describe how its beauty

killed his mother & taught him to hate applause.

Shadow Theatre

Not her hands or how they make the swan,
but its shadow & how it arches,

disturbs the pool of light without a ripple,
& turns slowly to face the children in love with swans

so they can see in its outline

the curved soliloquy that is the swan
in an illuminated field at their request.

The shadow resists a gold cage & the name "swan"

by how it unfurls, sweeps its one wing like a fan
impossible, perhaps, for swans

floating on an autumn lake amid red leaves,
shaking their heads at the coming frost

that will freeze into a single premise that
we must break to free the trapped swan,

crying of how its shadow revolves around its body
& outlasts all talk of swans.

Digital Archive

How should I index myself so that you can retrieve & cut me
　　　　from the 1970 catalogs

of infant headshots & paste me beside you?
　　　　This I wanted to know

while the grandfather held up his 1940 photo
　　　　of three men laughing beside a new Buick. He said,

"If you could identity them, then my life would be changed forever."
　　　　If anyone knows the names

for paper as vulnerable as skin, then please tell me
　　　　if I find my birth documents

burned, ripped, or yellowed with information missing,
　　　　or if I don't find them at all? I listened

as the panelists advised the grandfather to search the database,
　　　　my body like too much information

unsorted: all errors, useless without a way to see it
　　　　linked to get somewhere. My arms disappearing

while the grandfather passed his laminated photo around the room.

The Pavilion on Adams Avenue

Last month, they bulldozed the Barclay Hotel
established 1927, "50 Large Fireproof Rooms"
advertised on the east wall & once the avenue's finest
now tagged by Southside gangs & borrowed
by the homeless who bring their own blankets.

I watched the wrecking ball swing narrow
to knock through gas pipes, privacy
curtains of dust clearing away,
porcelain tubs crumbling with the brick edifice
dismantled for auction & scrap for a steel mill,

such that construction returned to fire to question,
How best to use a field cleared of debris?
Already they've erected a sign "Coming Soon:
Community Pavilion," cordoned off the site
piled with lumber. I've noticed on my morning walks

a new foundation measured & trussed with beams,
the promising outline of an entryway,
steps terraced to complement a garden,
eaves to extend the curvilinear bend of pines,
good ponds that guests will assume had always been there.

I can see barefoot lovers eating sandwiches in the corner
across from harbaji nostalgic for Namwan Pavilion,
his hands reassembling it before his grandchildren
listening while students hunch over notepads to copy
the slow ripple of a reed grove, swaying slope

Choson Dynasty monks exiled to mountains
discerned as an uneven basin.
They built mud walls that would not enclose the azaleas
but integrate their sprawl with autumn evenings
spent picking fleas off blankets.

Will there be bare wood brackets, interlocked columns
framing the eye's arrivals? I look forward to distance
just as Chong Chiyong who hiked the hilltop alone,
his lips gone dry & bitter with speaking of home
dwarfed by blue expanse.

Adrift in the familiar, he belonged among clouds.
Will this pavilion too allow us to recall the fugitive
chrysanthemums submitting roots to angled parapets
more natural than nature's dig toward water,
stone channels to float wine cups?

Unforeseen the number of visitors
who'll enter through here vistas of their own,
divided by what they long for & what they know
opposes such journeys toward zelkovas,
& the names of trees in another language, another clearing.

I assured my friend concerned with spelling
a pavilion does not decorate rather reveals
tensions between the false & real
shade of paulownias, inseparable as sunset
lengthening their shadows' dance, & when I go in

as my friend goes in, we'll be joined
by the ancient Chewoltang Pavilion, Taejojan Hall,
the Garden of Puyo, & Piwon Pavilion,
& the humble ones flooded & twisted with dandelions,
brothers to the secret ones we carry within.

Sijo

for omma

Outside your lit window, I stand ten thousand miles away.
Our distance shifts whenever you pass from room to room,
Whenever I pause from reading Kim So Wol's poetry.

On the beach

I walk among shells of star crabs
that failed to reach ocean
that reached for them with last night's tide.

Their attempts north remind
that home is not where one takes a lover
but longing for that lover

& in longing give witness
to snow-robed crags in morning fog,
an incense for sutras

to comfort the dead who must accept
a vault of ground
else they wander like an adopted child

dreaming the market streets of a mother
whose silence may be typical
traffic weaving through stalls, meats hung

above smoke cans, dogs searching wood
scents caught in the sleeves of grandmothers
schooled in fruit stands, eaves, stoops,

arguments over prices of watches,
the casualties of winter
war buried in a village's ditch, the lament I sing

for alleyways, the restaurant's backdoor
dumpsters boys dig through
for carrot peel & bones to run off with,

to scale chain linked fences hung with Hangul
signs I read as warnings
not to cross. My anthem, my pledged

allegiance to soldiers
stationed at the 38th parallel to keep uneasy peace,
my detente with

scowl-faced cab drivers,
who will drive me no where without overcharging
my white tongue

is untouchable, untouchable
as a young woman pregnant by a G.I.
turning on a baby's home cot toward a screened-in

window I do not look through for mother,
but her half moon
I follow through boulevards delivered to

courthouse steps,
cradle of abandoned children
not registered in the rolls of ancestors,

whose names are infinite. The whited-out
documents, my body the first & permanent.
I feel Korea – country of diaspora

like a pine cone crushed,
red seeds thrown from casing & eaten
or scattered by wind

into designs difficult to pronounce,
or spilled into sidewalk crevices
that choke saplings that would root anyway

though categories of fracture:
bastard, ghost, mix-blood, devil, illegitimate
love for this country

in which I am a reunion
broadcast aired nightly, my telethon for clues
leading to driveways,

or a ramshackle shack surrounded by barrels
to catch rainwater. My brother
is not there. My sister is not there

slicing persimmons & guessing
the dead sister no one speaks of lives on as me.
Her small knife pares skin

for the juiciest flesh that is not me. I take leave
from daybreak,
white sun like an egg cracked open,

yolk spread over post-war buildings, crowded teeth.
I cannot pass without pause
dead ends, banks, bars, agencies,

a father's bedroom
dutiful sons enter when asked
to pull afternoon drapes across

the fact of me
as apparent as the thief pocketing dried fish
& the vendor who yells, throws his hat.

No one helps him recover his loss.
No one speaks of this han, this legacy
like the constant pull of tides

on the shifting sand.
The ocean cleaves to shore
but cannot take it & recedes into memory,

so I could invent a Korea in the roaring
echoes of a conch shell I cup to my ear
to hear a stirring, familiar & foreign

currents of making that have nothing to do with
history's junked cargo of aliases,
x-rayed detritus, shriveled & still,

unremembered meanings
folded into locked drawers, files
I will not search.

My dream of resonance,
water answering distances. Like a peninsula,
I lie in spray & listen to everything borne.

V.

Where a chrysanthemum blooms then vanishes,
A chrysanthemum spirit arises and lives.
— So Chong Ju, "Ancient Song I"

KISAENG

"I want to understand the joy I felt
as I was letting him go."
—Hwang Jini

As I listened to the fabric of his jacket
      assume the casual shape of leave-taking,

I learned how to unhinge form from breath
      unbind & unknot the numinous black,

so that again I was a woman & an artist
      whose ravens fell onto the *ondol* floor

like cords, not a suicide's hair floating
      in a village well & souring the water.

Callus on my finger, cushion for the *kayabam*,
      we shall pluck the string to forget triumphs

before royalty taxing us for a celadon barge,
      shall sweep princes' names into a crevice

where we store besotted & sudden proposals
      to suck a jujube's succulent orb,

as if we required their directions to resist
      the stone in which a waiting life will crack

a rooting. Tendril of song, evening calm,
      guide my sense of use across the instrument

transforming my desire for vengeance
     into forest hearth smoke from which I fled

as a pretty child, selected by the king's men.
     Help me never to forget the elation I felt

when my first patron swore by the river's force
     his love for me, & I understood its swelling

to rush & breach could teach me to survive it
     by emptying myself to play a perfect note.

QUESTIONS FOR "A FLAME OF FIRE OUT OF A BUSH"

"Then Moses answered, 'But suppose
they do not believe me or listen to me…'"
— Exodus 4:1

How will my people recognize me —
a mumbler raised in the style of hunger

revivals, landlocked travel, long stretches of
porch talk to tell time by — as their prodigal,

their little, their follow, & watcher
of cues? How will they know me

by how I press my face to the floor
to behold my elder, my similar

bone structure softened by age
while I strain to raise myself upright?

How will they judge my open palms—
clutching or generous? Will that emptiness

translate? Will we require a looping
glance to confirm intent? To look away?

Is this a gesture of tenderness?
A scar? Should I hold back? What gift

of patience would they accept as winged,
not perused nor stolen?

How to present it? As somber, as joy?
What sign wired together, wrapped in foil

surely checked upon by someone
who is right? When does our silence

resonate? What honorary suffix,
or when I stutter, should someone else speak?

To apologize? To clarify? Should I
interrupt or answer? Or should I reach across

the lacquer table of cakes,
grasp their hands & guide them to my face

when they hesitate — uncertain how,
where to go, or what to do next?

Song Echoing Inside a Mountain Pavilion

You ask why such rage in my heart.
I'll let my arms be an answer of return

to your tender shadows, an aubade's fog
above inlets speckled with fishermen's cottages,

tethered boats loaded with nets checked for harvest
drawn from the river, the beautiful river,

my firstborn desire to dwell near its murmur.
I wake from dreaming one stone & finding one stone

remembered, & the names for one stone
remembered, & my tongue holding its syllabic heft

without effort, without conviction
so returning it to its proper place among others

flecked with salt & fixed in an upward stare
to where branches reach for each other in whispers.

What they say doesn't matter, but that I could rest
without checking every reference.

Little volumes of bushes, have I the right?
Chapters of fields, may I grieve? Titled ones...

My foothold, a footnote
for how to press my skin against yours,

cleave it from sources
anchoring my wandering mouth.

I'd take you without a shield, the visor that obscures
for the sake of progress

across your chest of unlikeness.
Hazardous twilight by which we perceive each other

by presence, unspoken but constant
as breathing & forgetting names for transport,

but musk will linger in our blue palanquin.
Your essence or the finest oil purchased?

That it could be approximated by doctors—
date of birth, mix of races, fixed, & unknown

by law— means that you are vulnerable to taste.
What are you? I recall your story:

From a street stand, your roommate selected by color
kumquat, star fruit, prickly pear, persimmon—

each one studied & savored. Hobbyist.
He chatted about hybrids (tangelos— his favorite).

"Try this," he said, holding out a sliver.
You bit into the nondescript flesh,

chased it with another slice then another
as your body crackled with recall, a mother

whose face you sensed but could not see.
Lying in bed, full beyond means, chin stained

by under-ripe fruit, you were like Proust
who ate madeleines till numbed by the taste.

Should you have rationed each one,
or does memory naturally lead to loss?

I love, so it's hard to tell
where Sukkul-am Cave is in *Pictorial Korea*.

Copyright 1956. The truth is purchased
from Pittsburgh's Caliban Bookshop in '99,

because the girl on the cover wore a striped hanbok.
She is me/is not me. (I'm learning

how to manage paradox.) She is smiling,
not for the camera, but somewhere unseen, now

behind her, a house out of focus. I don't know if
I'm a native stranger or strange native, or

is this tentative access? Loss, I need you
on pp. 120. Granite guardians watch those going in.

Those watched over are Guatama's guests.
Perhaps they want only to admire

his elaborately carved fingers, so intricate
they could take on without absolution

for each one: the student on holiday picnic
ties up her hair with a redbud scarf;

The old one in the corner rubbing his rosary;
he knows not what to think about requisitions.

About entering properly, you remind me
to place my hand over the face of the Deva King

to emphasize that I am a seeker
aware of those who came before & knelt.

I would walk out, but you scold me, take my papers.
You brush crumbs off my lank collar & spit

to rub off a smudge. I can't remember the last time
you told me not to slouch. Without a kiss,

this is tenderness. "Go ahead," you say without words,
without hesitation, & we enter a pavilion

quarried from & set in a mountain,
that takes it all back with saplings & overlooking

so much there is no history, save the wild turning
of vines across what could never be a home.

ELYSIAN FIELD

While soldiers check gates ridged with razor wire,
an eastern wind blows off the Sachon River holding the men
to routine stations & speeches blaring overhead.

The tallest flag in the world snaps back & forth
old caveats that flocks of ibis fly across

for wintering grounds seeded with landmines
still active from forty-five years ago when the gods
demarcated North from South & fortified towers

to play a new game of watch & wait.

All the while, maple, birch, & pine invaded the zone,
secured green shoots, & ringed many seasons
undisturbed as wild ginseng branched in understory.

It was dense enough for the white-bellied woodpecker
to drill a hole & nest, so too the black bear ambled
out of legend returning to rugged evergreen,

where it ignored the fairy pitta's shrill complaint
to white tigers once again trailing roe deer,

bowing their necks to chew new iris leaves.

*

How in the middle of hell is there a garden
of the unnamed & thought-to-be extinct

protected by danger?

Someone dressed casual breaks in, hides behind bushes,
whispers into a tape-recorder:

15 headed east, 22 southward. Maybe more.

Red-crowned & sleek, the cranes spring from the thickets

as if unhinging from a museum screen
landscape of bracken & a verse about happiness;

the watcher forgets though he learned in school
how the cities rose & pressed against mountains,
tore them down, then spilled over a grid of lights.

There is no light here except a distant detail

tracking the man tracking the cranes
flashing a signal as the flurry escapes. The squadron rushes in.

They throw the man spread-eagle down, search his jacket,
retrieve & rewind the scratched-up device:

. . .headed east, 22 southward. Maybe more.
15 headed east, 22 southward. Maybe. . .

They're listening. They want to know more.

*

I knew nothing, so all summer I read

sijo by an anonymous kisaeng

waiting for her secret lover to return from the north

until only her voice remained
fashioning a boat of giant pine to cross Taedong River,
& then her voice faded, but still the hull

was sturdy. I boarded it for wherever it would go
past the image of her breaking off a willow branch,

beyond jealous ones trying to pull her
headlong into quicksand.

The craft glided into her silence.

*

I disembark beside chrysanthemums,

& again, I see soldiers burn & slash the western forest
so they can spy on one another unobstructed.

Where trees fall, seedlings push through

& uncurl pale stalks beside tripwire
protecting them from harvest as medicine.

It's measure, not intention that saves

the rare & the beautiful. How innumerable
landmines defend against all sides,

so that in the center of violence, there is the impossible
green that peace might level.

Here, not irony nor survival. Wonder gives way
to life's drive toward transgressions
of root & petal. Here,

I must stop speaking; they may be listening
to trace my every movement

southward, east, or elsewhere. Take heart,

you still afraid of absence & myth,
my silence does not mean that I've disappeared.

River

My given name in Old English means "white wave,"
variant of Guenever, an adulteress,

so I too breach the binding cords
of the book to lay flat, reading the source of my adoption:

"choosing," origin French from Latin *adoptare*.

So the word resounds with travel across countries
to the present in which I drive

in my mind to the shore of forgetfulness.
Once, *Lethe* in Latin, & now, the pier from last night

I paced finding love everywhere

amorous on blankets, dejected in the stranger throwing letters
into high tide, in the disappearing sandals

someone forgot to move to higher ground.

It's all coming back to me now.

What else do we inherit but choice,
not to go near the water or to plunge into surf,

or not to choose at all

when the law says there is only one way to hunger & to thirst?

*

It's all coming back to me now
in an Antonioni film about a photographer

beautiful as *don't-try-to-impress-me* in creased, white pants.

He drags off a cigarette, cocked sixties-style, because
he can.

He wants to see through the smoke, jones, & sentiment,
the dripping black & white

image clothes pinned to string,
the same image blown up again & again &...

He's looking for a way past the ink surface.

Underneath an extreme lens,
the blur comes into focus as volatile

particles that take on an outline

of a form running from a field cleared of trees,

which must be some scene of transgression, or why
is one running, or what

about the image's grain bears a trace?

*

How can it be pinned down when it's constantly moving?

Because the story of how Omma died depends
on who tells the story,

how it ends with her body irretrievable among twisted, car metal
or forever violated

by the accurate work of a court transcriber or—

I choose the negative space among the dark, magnified bits
that is not a silence

but an opening to slip through these stories into the possible
where she is not all body,

as if hunger is a child wanting back inside

rocking water & the crimson interior of her
name & the names given by lovers & anonymous ones.

What child can count them all on his fingers,

when not to know is to have her more

as myth from which we all descend
or must confront for the source of making?

✻

While my mother read aloud from the yellowed *Aeneid*,
dog-eared & spine broken, I felt my body transform

to pass through her pauses & turning the page, & the page turning against the Oklahoma midnight & star luster.

The pages turning into an infinite white blur,
a gate to the shores of the river.

Her voice working left to right across

long sentences of preparation
(how the hero broke off a gold branch to bribe the boatman)
& returning to the subject of descent

into the underside of the garland strewn field, cleared of trees.

Someone running for help, while she read aloud.

Someone disappearing as I walked.

I carried her voice.
It knocked inside my ear, checked my gestures.

"Do not. Do not go near the water. Do not Do not,"
a pace for footsteps

behind a crag, a shielded look-out

to the boat tied to the dock,
the unburied souls wandering up & down the swamp.

"Empty images
hovering bodiless" hungry for a little earth to cover them
begged the boatman for passage.

I studied each one for my loss. I did not find her

in the deformed face of the suicide,
did not recognize the wound
in the little mother's arm or

the bent one whose steel hair drug the ground.

The austere red of the widow resisted me,
& I felt nothing

but compassion
for the one pulling at her braids

or the old ones forever

stumbling through a blasted camp,
wide-eyed, as if seeing life for the first time
riddled by open air fire; & the one
crouching in the gutter while caissons roll
north & south; & the one thrown by a landmine

shaking handfuls of roots like fistfuls of dice.

*

They want to be buried, to be forgotten properly.
They want it though the living may not

string garlands, tune instruments, or choose

a field of grass gleaming like water.

What does one represent but a failure
to stand for all the names hovering bodiless,
pressing their claims for transport?

How does one turn away from their calling?

✲

How could I forget at the beach's edge,

a mound of twisted kelp laid on its side
as the tides rolled in to pull it apart, rolled in pulling

like midnight hands across a clock-face

to deny it body & so drag it back into the black water?

But its knots moved like sinew with the currents;
moved with, not against, & so stayed

in a bed of sand carved out by undercurrents
lifting it gently on to the bed.

Impassive, its leaves undulated in the slow swirling,
rose & fell, rose & fell, & I could see,

exposed to moonlight,
not a tangle of leaves but a letting go

of names that would weigh down its body
like cargo buoyed far then forever lost.

I can't bear this, can't stop

translating her body by water to move it again & again &...

not Omma, now mother, now the Indo-European root,
now the sharing

by Latin *mater* & the Greek

mētēr, not measure's source yet I count
back to *mater*, the heart of matter,

matter with a heart, *māternus*, & every material

bearing her trace,

bearing her variously   in the grain of everything

Variation on "Azaleas"

Little one, though you go away
because you cannot bear with me,

one day you will search
the graves of ancestors

not for my name, but for yourself
to find the azaleas of Yaksan Hill.

Surely, I will never see you again.
I will not weep,
because I can imagine you are

a grandfather
who slips off his sandals to tread gently
on the flowers across Yaksan Hill.

NOTES ON THE POEMS

"A Small Gift" is for Ku Sang, a modern Korean poet. Some of the fourth line's language is from his long poem, "River and Fields." My poem tonally enacts Korean *han*, which is difficult to explain in English. Its meaning is close to "wounded heart" but "enduring," and not just "enduring" but finding some hope and happiness even in struggling.

I draw from Thomas Park Clement's *The Unforgotten War* to trigger "Homage to the DMZ." This poem is for him. In the Korean story, a woman waiting for her beloved to return becomes an anemone, which is slumped over and has gray hair touching the ground. In this way, the anemone represents nostalgia or endless waiting.

"Elegy for Daniel" is for the memory of Daniel Anderson and his unpublished book, *Red Cracked Earth.*

The epigraph for "Libretto" is from Cio-Cio-San's final aria in *Madama Butterfly* Act 2: "Never know that, for you, / Butterfly is about to die… The next few lines complete her thought: "so that you may go / away beyond the sea / without being subject to remorse / in later years / for your mother's desertion."

"Painted Fire" is triggered by *Chihwaseon,* a film about the life of Chang Sung-Op (Ohwon) who is the last significant artist of the Yi Dynasty, and alludes to his painting titled "Eagles." Since according to the *Shih Ching* "poetry is art, and art is poetry," Korean artists conventionally included poetry within their paintings and oftentimes responded to poems in the moment of their artwork's creation. The quotes in "Painted Fire" are from the Tao Chien's "Homecoming," which set the moment of composition for Ohwon's "Eagles."

Etymologically, *sijo* is a combination of two Sino-Korean characters meaning "time" or "period" and "rhythm" or "harmony." In an introduction to *Classical Korean Poetry*, Kim Jaihiun offers a prosodic and historical overview of the sijo, or "song of seasons" as it has been called:

> The *sijo* is a traditional lyric of three lines or verses averaging 45 syllables in a stanza, each line made up of four phrase-groupings with a major pause after each grouping. This is not exactly the same as a caesura in English verse because it cannot be syncopated with metric feet . . . Extremely elastic in form, the *sijo* differs from Chinese and Japanese verse forms in that it does not adhere to a strict syllable account. (xix)

The *sijo* consists of three lines. The first one states the poem's occasion, and the third one answers, resolves, or comments on it. In this way, the third line is a kind of *volta*. Recent translations of *sijo* sometimes break each line apart midway by way of enjambment in order to signal this major pause in English. This topography may imply that the *sijo* is a sestet or, without the line breaks, a tercet. It is neither.

The quotes in "Kameoka" are from translations of Matsuo Basho's haiku and "Saga Diary," both of which are anthologized in Robert Hass's *Haiku: Versions of Basho, Buson, and Issa*. Kameoka is a city in Kyoto Prefecture, Japan. This poem is for Kumiko Watanabe.

The opening lines of "Prodigal" are a variation on Matsuo Basho's haiku, "Even in Kyoto/ I long for Kyoto/ ." In the 15th C, King Sejong developed *Hunmin chong'um* (also known as *Onmun* and now generally known as *Hangul*) or "Correct Sounds for Educating the People" as a way to combat illiteracy. Initially, the women at court primarily used the Korean language since the men continued to employ Chinese as the language of art, culture, and diplomacy.

"Paperclips" refers to *zuihitsu* in Kimiko Hahn's *The Unbearable Heart*. The *zuihitsu*, or "running brush," is a Japanese form made up of short prosaic moments wandering from subject to subject and enacting a spontaneous and fluid mind. Sei Shonagon's *Pillow Book* is one such classical example.

Kim So Wol (1902-1935) wrote during the Independence Movement and is considered one of Korea's finest modern poets. His book, *Jindallae-kkot*, is a benchmark in the development of Korea's literary heritage. The widely anthologized title poem carries nationalist force given its underlying sacrificial suffering attitude to life occasioned by the Japanese occupation. I am grateful to Kim So Wol's family—Unhae Langis and Patrick and Nancy Park—for sharing their insights and translations of his poetry.

"Authenticity" is for Malcolm Fitzgerald Cash and his creative nonfiction.

The poet, Chong Chiyong, is a Korean modernist, and I quote from his poem "Native Village" in "The Pavilion on Adams Avenue."

The *kisaeng* were women artists trained in fine arts and literature, employed by the state, and considered inferior in social status. Their poetry survives despite the fact that many of their names have been forgotten. Hwang Jini, a 16th century *kisaeng*, is considered the most famous due to her great poetic skill and intellect.

The first line from "Song Echoing Inside a Mountain Pavilion" refers to the opening line in David St. John's poem "Nervalesque" from *Red Leaves of Night*. Deva Kings (or the guardians of the four directions — North, South, East, and West) guard the entryways of Buddhist temples.

In the language of birds, the crane symbolizes happiness. In the language of flowers, the chrysanthemum belongs to poets. The *sijo* of anonymous *kisaeng*, or "artist women," referred to in "Elysian Field" are from *Classical Korean Poetry* edited and translated by Jaihiun Kim.

The opening of "River" is after Larry Levis's "The Two Trees" in *Elegy*.

The poem through which "Variation" is written is Kim So Wol's "Azaleas," and I dedicate it to Kelly Ahern.

■ ■

With endless love and gratitude to David St. John, Norman Dubie, Carol Muske Dukes, James Kincaid, Susan McCabe, Viet Thanh Nguyen, Roberto Ignacio Diaz, Nick Carbo, Fiona Cheong, Kwame Dawes, Lynn Emanuael, Lisa Lewis, Marianne Novy, Ed Ochester, Frank Ticheli, and to Larry Levis's poetry.

I am indebted to Chris Abani, Aimee Beal, Ava Chin, Ashley Currier, Kristin Herbert Fisher, Steve and Colleen Gates, Laura Johnson, Unhae Langis, Charles Ilwoo Lee, L. Alvis Minor, r.r., Eric Rawson, P.B. Rippey, and Amy Newlove Schroeder, whose artistic genorosity and insights helped to build a pavilion.

About Jennifer Kwon Dobbs

Jennifer Kwon Dobbs was born in Won Ju, South Korea. Her poems have appeared in or forthcoming from *5 AM, Crazyhorse, Cimarron Review, Cream City Review, MiPOesias, Poetry NZ, Tulane Review,* among others and has been anthologized in *Echoes Upon Echoes* (Temple University Press 2003) and *Contemporary Voices from the Eastern World* (W. W. Norton 2008). She is Edwin Mem Fellow at the University of Southern California and founding director of the SummerTIME Writing Program. She lives in Los Angeles and New York.

Author photograph by Dave Cochran Photography.

THE WHITE PINE PRESS POETRY PRIZE

Vol. 12   Paper Pavilion by Jennifer Kwon Dobbs
           Selected by Genie Zeiger

Vol. 11   *The Trouble with a Short Horse in Montana* by Roy Bentley
           Selected by John Brandi

Vol. 10   *The Precarious Rhetoric of Angels* by George Looney
           Selected by Nin Andrews

Vol. 9   *The Burning Point* by Frances Richey
           Selected by Stephen Corey

Vol. 8   *Watching Cartoons Before Attending A Funeral* by John Surowiecki
           Selected by C.D. Wright

Vol. 7   *My Father Sings, To My Embarrassment* by Sandra Castillo
           Selected by Cornelius Eady

Vol. 6   *If Not For These Wrinkles of Darkness* by Stephen Frech
           Selected by Pattiann Rogers

Vol. 5   *Trouble in History* by David Keller
           Selected by Pablo Medina

Vol. 4   *Winged Insects* by Joel Long
           Selected by Jane Hirshfield

Vol.3   *A Gathering of Mother Tongues* by Jacqueline Joan Johnson
           Selected by Maurice Kenny

Vo. 2   *Bodily Course* by Deborah Gorlin
           Selected by Mekeel McBride

Vol. I   *Zoo & Cathedral* by Nancy Johnson
           Selected by David St. John